The Gulf of St Lawrence

(overleaf) *CN Marine ferry to Port aux Basques, Nfld*

The Gulf of St Lawrence

By Harry Bruce
Wayne Barrett and Anne MacKay

Toronto
OXFORD UNIVERSITY PRESS
1984

ACKNOWLEDGEMENTS

We would like to thank the many people who have
helped us in our work on this book, including
Roger Cameron and CN Marine, The Canadian Coast
Guard, the Federal Department of Fisheries and
Oceans, Pierre Bertrand, and Duncan MacCormick, of
Anticosti Island; finally and especially David Webber
who suggested the idea of such a book in the first place.

Quotations attributed to Jacques Cartier are taken from
The Voyages of Jacques Cartier (Ottawa, 1924) ed. by H.P. Biggar.

Bruce, Harry, 1934–

The Gulf of St Lawrence

ISBN 0-19-540452-1

1. St Lawrence, Gulf of—description and travel.
I. Barrett, Wayne. II. MacKay, Anne. III. Title.

FC 2004. B78 1984   917. 1'096 344   C84-098394-8
F 1050. B 78 1984

Produced by Roger Boulton Publishing Services, Toronto
Designed by Fortunato Aglialoro (Studio 2 Graphics)
© Oxford University Press (Canadian Branch) 1984
OXFORD is a trademark of Oxford University Press
ISBN 0-19-540452-1

1 2 3 4 - 7 6 5 4

Printed in Hong Kong by Scanner Art Services, Inc., Toronto

Introduction

RINGED BY FIVE of Canada's ten provinces, the Gulf of St Lawrence is the ocean entryway to an entire continent. From Strait of Belle Isle, the Gulf's northernmost approach from the open Atlantic, vessels penetrate 2,045 miles up the St Lawrence system—past Montreal, Toronto, Cleveland and Detroit; past the longitudes of Boston, New York, Pittsburgh and Chicago—all the way west to Duluth, Minnesota. Explorers and traders once pushed onward by canoe. They followed other rivers out to the mountains of the far west, north to the Arctic Ocean, and all the way south to the Gulf of Mexico. These forays to the very limits of an unknown continent remain part of the upriver epic. The downriver story is no less dramatic. In peace, war, settlement and trade, the St Lawrence has borne outbound vessels as surely as it has flowed to the Gulf, and on to the sea. Since the age of Martin Luther, Michelangelo, and the Spanish conquistadors, the river and its Gulf have been highway and harbour to the sailors of the world.

No one will ever know when the first sea-going vessel from Europe penetrated the Gulf. Some have concocted bizarre theories that Phoenicians and ancient Romans actually reached North America. Some believe that the Micmac Indians, who knew the Gulf when Christ walked the earth, are descendants of Mediterranean peoples. Maybe St Brendan, the Sinbad of Ireland, really did sail his leather boat to the Gulf in the sixth century AD. Maybe Henry Sinclair, a Scottish prince, really did spend a year in Nova Scotia a century before Columbus 'discovered' America. And maybe the Vikings had reached the Gulf centuries before that. The remains of their thousand-year-old settlement at L'Anse-aux-Meadows, Newfoundland, overlook the seaward entrance to Strait of Belle Isle; and it's unlikely that a people whose daring had brought them so far would not have popped through the strait to the waters beyond.

In 1497 skipper John Cabot, probably of Genoa but sailing under the English flag, made a North American landfall, perhaps at the southwestern corner of Newfoundland, perhaps at the northern tip of Cape Breton Island, Nova Scotia. In either case, he reached the strait that now bears his name without ever learning that it led to the great Gulf, and beyond that to the great river. Later explorers also ranged along the coast, from Labrador to New England, without sailing either southwest through Strait of Belle Isle or northwest through Cabot Strait. It was left to Jacques Cartier, from St Malo in France, to discover the Gulf as an 'official' explorer in 1534.

By then, however, trans-Atlantic voyages were routine for the tough, anonymous fishermen of western England, France, Spain, Portugal and the country of the Basques, and 'the man from St Malo' was by no means the first European of his time to sail the Gulf. But the fact that he discovered the already-discovered scarcely detracts from his immortal achievement. On that first of his three voyages to Canada, he didn't merely visit the Gulf, he investigated it, described it, felt it out as no one had ever done before. Between early June of 1534, when he entered Strait of

Belle Isle, and his departure through the same passage in mid-August, he cruised the west coast of Newfoundland, the northwest corner of Prince Edward Island, the east coast of New Brunswick and Chaleur Bay, the Gaspé coast, and hundreds of miles of Quebec's Lower North Shore. During this mighty loop round most of the Gulf's perimeter, he also inspected the Magdalen Islands and almost entirely circled the massive Anticosti Island.

A good summer's work, 450 years ago.

Like explorers before him, and explorers for generations after, Cartier was driven by the most powerful obsession in the history of navigation—the dream of finding a short, safe route across the western ocean to the silks, spices and fabulous wealth that lay in trade with the Far East. Just one shipload of nutmeg and pepper could make a man rich for life, and the dream tempted many a captain beyond the edge of the known world. But if Cartier was a dreamer, he was also an observant dreamer, a reporter, a trader, a negotiator. There was a practical, crafty side to his daring, and his second voyage, which took him all the way upriver to Montreal, confirmed him forever as the man who showed old France the path to New France. He unlocked the Gulf, but the keys to its future would not be cloves and cinnamon. They'd be furs, fish, timber, the cannon and the cross.

For two centuries after Cartier's voyages, the cannon often seemed dominant. From beyond the Gulf even to the Mississippi, conflict between the imperial ambitions of France and Britain fumed, smouldered, periodically exploded in flames and gore. The Gulf lay between the continent's heart and the Newfoundland fisheries. It was New France's ocean buffer and maritime outpost; but its eastern wall was Newfoundland, and that lay like 'a great English ship moored near the fishing banks.' In 1759, the British captured Quebec City. In 1760, they demolished Fortress Louisbourg, the walled town that the French had built on Ile-Royale (Cape Breton Island) near the Cabot Strait. France was now finished in the Gulf, and so was major warfare.

Vessels have since carried men and munitions over the Gulf and onward to cataclysms around the world, but it has not been an important theatre of war itself. 'The Battle of the St Lawrence', for instance, was just a sideshow of World War II in a sparsely populated, sub-arctic byway of the northwest Atlantic. But, for the people of the Gulf and the lower river, it was grim enough. Nazi U-boats roamed their waters for five months in 1942, sank 23 ships, killed 700 people. That was more people than the Canadian Army lost in Sicily.

Only a few hundred thousand people live in communities scattered around the Gulf's long, intricate coast—much of it as wild as it was when Cartier first saw it— and its human history is mostly a quiet saga of survival. Its natural history, however, is spectacular. The Gulf lies smack in the middle of one of the world's great flyways for migratory birds. No spring passes without the sight and din of wave upon wave of southbound landbirds. No autumn passes without mighty invasions of north-bound shorebirds. Gulf waters surround island sanctuaries for fabulous and some-times deafening colonies of seabirds. As fisheries, parts of the Gulf rival the offshore banks, and early every winter hordes of seals ride floating ice down through Strait of Belle Isle to whelp near the Magdalen Islands. Whales romp in Gulf waters, and its coasts are home to every creature from bears to hares, from deer to doormice, from wolves to woodchucks, from cats to caribou.

The Gulf is no mere river mouth. With an area of 60,000 square miles, it's half as big as the Baltic Sea. The river, which drains 500,000 square miles of hinterland, dumps fresh water into the Gulf from the southwest, while the ocean pumps in salt water from the northeast. The Gulf contains 35,000 cubic miles of water, but powerful currents and the pull of the earth's rotation combine to change the entire contents every two years and four months. Cutting across the bed of this inland sea, running from the continental shelf all the way up to the mouth of the Saguenay River, is the Laurentian Channel. A testament to the gouging power of ancient glacial action, it has depths of 250 fathoms.

The Gulf endures wild extremes. Not 300 miles separate its northern and southern limits, yet the north may be suffering an Arctic blizzard while the south experiences only a muggy fog, broken with flashes of sunlight. In northern New Brunswick and the Gaspé, the temperature may soar to 100°F in summer and plummet to −40°F in winter. Calm days on Gulf waters are rarer than pearls, but gales last for days on end. The Gulf is violent, diverse, unpredictable.

Such a place deserves a respectful approach, from a respectful distance. For the purpose of this book then, the inland limits of the Gulf are well upriver at Isle d'Orléans, the tidal divide where outbound vessels first come to terms with the ocean's pull; and the outer limits begin off Newfoundland's Atlantic coasts, where vessels jammed with gritty, hopeful people have been pushing westward to the Gulf for God alone knows how many years.

Four-hundred-and-fifty at the very least.

Halifax, February, 1984   HARRY BRUCE

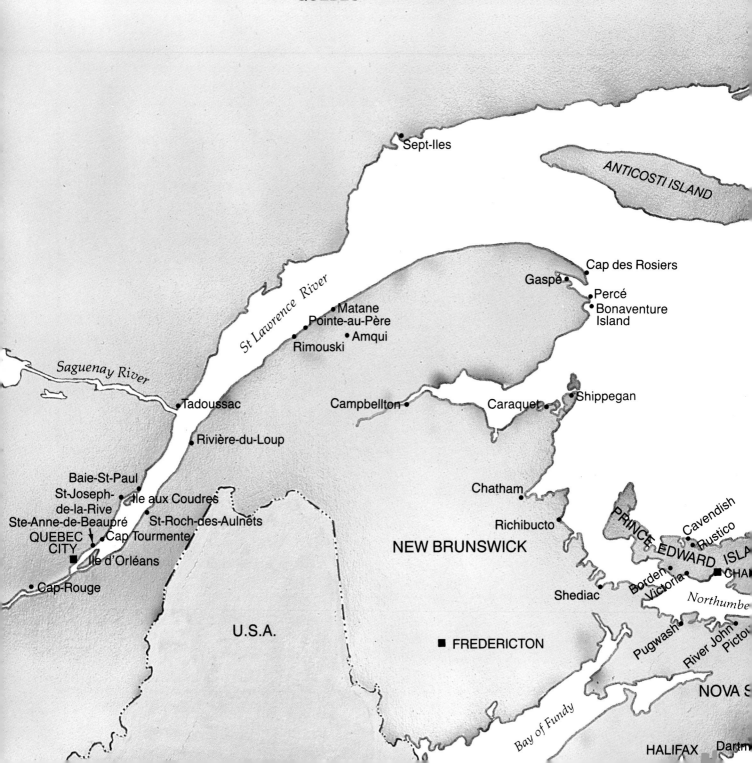

QUEBEC

Sept-Iles

ANTICOSTI ISLAND

Cap des Rosiers

Gaspé

Percé

Bonaventure
Island

St Lawrence River

Matane
Pointe-au-Père
Amqui
Rimouski

Saguenay River

Tadoussac

Campbellton

Caraquet

Shippegan

Rivière-du-Loup

Baie-St-Paul
St-Joseph-
de-la-Rive
Ste-Anne-de-Beaupré
QUEBEC
CITY

Île aux Coudres

St-Roch-des-Aulnets

Cap Tourmente

Île d'Orléans

Cap-Rouge

Chatham

Richibucto

NEW BRUNSWICK

PRINCE

Cavendish

Rustico

EDWARD ISLA

CHA

Borden
Victoria
Northumbe

Shediac

U.S.A.

■ FREDERICTON

Pugwash

River John

Pictou

Bay of Fundy

NOVA S

HALIFAX   Dartm

LABRADOR

Blanc-Sablon

Pistolet Bay

L'Anse aux Meadows

St Anthony

ATLANTIC OCEAN

Strait of Belle Isle

LONG RANGE MOUNTAINS

Harrington
Harbour

Rocky
Harbour

*GROS
MORNE
NATIONAL
PARK*

Bonne Bay

Trout River

Corner
Brook

NEWFOUNDLAND

ST. JOHN'S

Grand Bruit

Burgeo

Francois

Harbour
Breton

BURIN PENINSULA

CAPE
RACE

CAPE
RAY

Rose Blanche

Ramea

C. ST. MARY'S

Channel-
Port aux
Basques

Isle aux Morts

ST PIERRE
AND MIQUELON

ST PIERRE

Bird Rock
Island

Cabot Strait

agdalen Islands
s de la Madeleine)

St Lawrence

héticamp

*CAPE
BRETON
HIGHLANDS
NATIONAL
PARK*

Mabou

North Sydney

*CAPE BRETON
ISLAND*

ulgrave

Arichat

Strait of Canso

ATLANTIC OCEAN

1 *Sunrise over the Gulf on one of those rare, calm days*

2 & 3 *Cape Race, Nfld*

AT THE SOUTHEAST TIP of Newfoundland's Avalon Peninsula, a jumble of jagged cliffs challenges the
Atlantic Ocean. They are Cape Race, the first land
that most Gulf-bound ships from Europe spot on their
way west. Once they've come within sight of the Cape
Race lighthouse, skippers know that, to reach the
Gulf beyond the south coast of Newfoundland, they
must leave to their starboard a mere 500 kilometres of
the most treacherous rock in the world. Odds are
they'll have to contend with storms, fogs or icebergs,
as well. The lighthouse sits atop 100-foot-high cliffs,
and rises a further 96 feet. When it was built to replace
an earlier tower in 1907, lighthouse authorities ranked
it among the best in the world. The cast iron, steel
framing, copper dome, lens, prisms and other ingredi-
ents of the signalling apparatus, and all its housing at
the tower's peak, weighed no less than 42 tons, including seven tons of optical equipment floating on a 950-
lb. bath of mercury. This was a champion among
lighthouses. The men who counted upon it deserved
no less.

4 & 5 (overleaf) *St Mary's, Nfld*

'WAIT A FAIR WIND,' advises an old Newfoundland saying, 'and you'll get one.' Here, it's St Mary's
on the Avalon Peninsula that's getting fair weather.
Another Newfoundland saw asserted that the nearby
fisheries were so prolific that 'Cape St Mary's pays for
all.'

6 *St Anthony, Nfld*

THE HOSPITAL PLANE of the Grenfell Mission is a familiar sight not only here at mission headquarters in St Anthony, near the tip of the Great Northern Peninsula, but also in more isolated outports in northern Newfoundland and Labrador. The mission provides medical aid for 2,400 kilometres of forbidding coastline, and maintains a network of nursing stations and clinics. Sir Wilfred Grenfell (1865–1940), a man of fanatical dedication, was an extraordinary character in the extraordinary history of Newfoundland. He was a doctor, author, social worker, and zealot, and brought evangelical fervour to his lifelong campaign to improve the lives and health of the half-starved fishing families he first met in 1892.

7 (right) *Harbour Breton, Nfld*

ON THE SOUTH COAST of Newfoundland, a fellow learns the ways of the water early in life.

MAN AND BOY out for a spin at McCallum on the barren, intricate, south coast of Newfoundland. Describing coastal Newfoundland in 1899, an Ontario-born writer named Agnes Laut marvelled that, 'Generations of the people have never seen cattle. A cow would be regarded with much the same awe that a hippopotamus might cause; and there is neither path nor pasturage for a horse. . . . The sea is the fisherman's highway, and when he wishes to pay a friendly visit across the lagoon, punt or dory is unmoored.' For many, the sea is still the highway, and the only pastures are still the grazing grounds of fish. If you keep this grim shore on your starboard side for long enough, you'll pop out into the Gulf.

8 *McCallum, Nfld*

9 *L'Anse aux Meadows, Nfld*

HERE AT L'ANSE AUX MEADOWS, Newfoundland, at the tip of the Great Northern Peninsula, near the most northerly entrance to the Gulf, lie the remains of a settlement that Vikings occupied some 500 years before Columbus sailed the ocean blue. No one has yet proved that this eerie spot is the location of the lost 'Vinland' that the legendary Leif Ericsson discovered, but it's indisputable that Vikings lived here around AD 1000. They apparently stayed about 25 years. It was Norwegian archaeologists Helge and Anne-Stine Ingstad who, after careful reading of the ancient Icelandic sagas, began to dig in the bog and grassland at L'Anse-aux-Meadows in 1961. What they found—the earliest known settlement of Europeans in North America—inspired the United Nations, in 1980, to proclaim the ruins a World Heritage Site.

A FISHERMAN AT FRANCOIS has no shortage of fair-weather friends. If cod are the goats of the deeps, herring gulls are the goats of the coastline. They eat virtually anything, and they're proliferating on almost every Atlantic shoreline. They share the Gulf with small Bonaparte's gulls, black-headed gulls from Europe, and ring-billed gulls from the Mississippi. The great, black-backed gull, noticeable in the mob pictured here, has changed from being a winter resident to a year-rounder that accounts for at least ten per cent of gull flocks in the Gulf.

10 *Francois, Nfld*

11 *St Anthony, Nfld*

12 *Harbour Breton, Nfld*

OUTPORTS LIKE HARBOUR BRETON cling to rock for the sake of fish all along Newfoundland's south coast. Here it's the ocean that's fertile, never the land. There's a theory that thousands of years ago southbound glaciers bulldozed Newfoundland's soil into the ocean and thereby created the banks that lure fishing fleets from a dozen countries on two continents. If the theory's true, the fertility of the sea is the lost fertility of the island.

13 *Grand Bruit, Nfld*

AS WESTBOUND VESSELS approach Cabot Strait to enter the Gulf, they leave Burgeo to starboard, and also Ramea, Grand Bruit, Rose Blanche, and other outports that are forever caught, as the saying goes, between a rock and a hard place. The rock is obvious. The hard place is the sea. In July 1828 the brig *Dispatch*, bound from Londonderry to Quebec with 200 passengers and nine crew, passed Grand Bruit in a blinding fog and, further west, turned north to enter the Gulf. She turned too soon and cracked up on a reef near a spot that still bears the morbidly appropriate name of Isle-aux-Morts (Island of Corpses).

For every looter of wrecks there was also a hero of wrecks. Fisherman George Harvey, the first settler in those parts, an aging father of eight children, stumbled on the disaster. Taking a seventeen-year-old daughter, a twelve-year-old son and, as tradition has it, a dog with him in a punt, Harvey managed to help save 163 men, women and children from the wreck.

14 *Corner Brook, Nfld*

FOREST HARVEST, Corner Brook, inland from the
Gulf coast of Newfoundland.

15 (right) *Burgeo, Nfld*

NEAR BURGEO, the air can be gentle and the sea
benign. But on other days in another century—on this
same busy, grisly, south coast of Newfoundland—
storms routinely demolished big vessels on their way
to and from the Gulf. Widow-making weather struck
shipping with such regularity that the impoverished
folk on the shore came to see loot from 'wracks', and
from the corpses of the drowned, as rightful gifts from
God.

16 *Pistolet Bay, Nfld*

BEFORE CROSSING Strait of Belle Isle to Labrador, you cannot get much further north in Newfoundland than Pistolet Bay.

17 (right) *Harbour Breton, Nfld*

FISHING OFF NEWFOUNDLAND is a multimillion-dollar business for some, just an income supplement for others, a form of subsistence farming for still others. Here at Harbour Breton, near the southern route from Europe to the gulf, an assortment of boats shares one purpose: catching fish.

THE GULF AT TIMES still manages to isolate two entire provinces, and ferries must struggle to re-establish the link with mainland Canada. Ferries of CN Marine sail between Port Aux Basques, Nfld., pictured here, and North Sydney, N.S. They thus cross Cabot Strait, the widest entrance to the Gulf, serve as a sea-going extension of the Trans-Canada Highway, and link Newfoundland to the rest of the country.

CN Marine performs the same service for Prince Edward Island with its Northumberland Strait boats. The Micmacs, the French settlers, and the first Irish farmers of P.E.I. could not possibly have imagined, not in their wildest midnight fantasies, the power and safety of the ferries that now cross Northumberland Strait. For 142 years—from the time of the American revolution right down to the First World War—men used skiffs, canoes, and dories in scheduled charges over the booby traps of ice and paralysing water that lay between them and the far shore. They ran risks at which mountain-climbers and Arctic explorers would not sneer, routinely performing feats of endurance that would challenge the wind and shake the courage of even the most fit among today's outdoorsmen. Some lost fingers, feet, even their lives for the glory of the 'ice-boat' service, but in most Canadian history books they fail to make even the footnotes.

A measure of their achievement is the fact that, even now—despite bow propellers, heavy steel plate, ship-to-shore phones, electronic navigation, precise charts, and diesel power—there are winter days when ferryboat skippers consider the state of the Strait and decide that prudence is the better part of seamanship. They cancel the odd voyage.

18 *Port aux Basques, Nfld*

19 *Rocky Harbour, Nfld*

AS THE SUN SLIDES INLAND, hundreds of light-houses—scattered along thousands upon thousands of miles of coastline in five provinces—start to blink their reassurance across the waters of the Gulf to freighters, tankers, ferries, and fishing boats. In its own way, each lighthouse says the same thing: 'Here I am . . . Here I am.' For navigators, that's an important statement. Gulf weather can be vicious and fickle. It can suddenly turn not merely violent, but deceptive as well. Losing your way can kill you. This lighthouse is at Rocky Harbour, Bonne Bay, in Gros Morne National Park, western Newfoundland. The Park faces the Gulf for forty miles. The flat-topped Long Range Mountains brood above a coastal plain, and split here and there to accommodate fiords of Norwegian majesty. The mountains are almost inconceivably ancient. Scientists say the base rocks are more than 1,500 million years old.

20 & 21 (overleaf) *Gros Morne National Park, Nfld*

IN GEOLOGICAL TIME the period since 1534, when Jacques Cartier first saw these lowering palisades of rock, amounts only to a blink of God's eye. The Long Range Mountains on the Gulf shore of Newfoundland haven't had time to change since then. If Cartier could return, he'd still know them. He went on from there that summer to find the Magdalen Islands, Prince Edward Island, the Gulf coast of New Brunswick, Chaleur Bay, the Gaspé Peninsula, Anticosti Island, and much of the northern shore of the Gulf; and he still managed to get home to St Malo, France, well before snow fell either there or in the colder territory he'd just claimed for the King of France. Like a returning bird, he was back in the Gulf the following spring, and this time he followed the St Lawrence River all the way up to Montreal.

23 *Iles de la Madeleine, Qué.*

JACQUES CARTIER found the Iles de la Madeleine (Magdalen Islands) in 1534, and their sparkle so impressed him he said two acres of them were worth more than all Newfoundland. He hadn't seen them in winter. That's Ile-d'Entrée in the photo and, if you can believe it, it's as far south as Paris. The Magdalens lie seventy miles off the north-east tip of Prince Edward Island, 160 miles from Quebec. Administratively, they're part of Quebec. Linguistically, they're primarily French. Most of the 13,500 islanders are descendants of Acadians who fled British rule in Nova Scotia after 1755, but nearly a thousand are English-speaking descendants of Cape Breton Scots, and survivors of shipwrecks.

Sand dunes and ramparts of red rock join six of the seven islands that humans inhabit, as opposed to birds, but the seventh is literally stand-offish. Ile-d'Entrée is out in the Gulf to the east of the main archipelago, and that's where a few hundred of the English-speaking Magdalen islanders somehow survive the winters all by themselves. Some of them, sometimes, may wish they were in a warm place like Newfoundland.

22 (left) *Road to Trout River, Nfld*

THE BARRENNESS of the Serpentine Tableland in Newfoundland's Gros Morne National Park is almost lunar. The icy beauty thrills some, makes others shudder, and the landscape is no more inviting in summer. With the snow gone, plains, cliffs, and ram- parts of brown, treeless rock stand naked in the wind. This road leads over the shoulder of Tabletop Mountain, down to the village of Trout River, and so to a dead end on the shingle beach of the Gulf.

STONE IS SOFT and winter hard on the Magdalen Islands.

24 *Iles de la Madeleine, Qué.*

25 *St Pierre, St Pierre and Miquelon*

IS THIS A NEWFOUNDLAND OUTPORT, a town in north-eastern New Brunswick, a riverside community in Quebec? Guess again. It is, in fact, St Pierre of St Pierre and Miquelon, conspicuous specks of France that dangle within sight of the south coast of Newfoundland. St Pierre is home to 6,000 citizens of France. No one knows precisely when Basque and Breton fishermen first used the archipelago as summer headquarters, but French fishermen appear to have settled there in the early 1600s and, except for two British interruptions, it's been French territory since 1635. Three-and-a-half centuries later the fact of its Frenchness threatened relationships between Canada and France over the issue of territorial rights to off-shore oil.

26 *La Roncière, St Pierre*

LIKE MARTINIQUE AND GUADELOUPE, away to the south in the Caribbean, St Pierre and Miquelon are tiny remnants of the French empire in the New World. The atmosphere of Old France still lingers in St Pierre. It's a place of fresh breads and faded paint, of lace, dust, and flowers in windows, of red wine, white cheese, and blue ocean waters.

27 *St Pierre*

THE POST OFFICE at St Pierre, France's stone tidbit
in the southern sealanes to the Gulf.

28 *Restaurant 'Le Joinville', St Pierre*

THOUGH ST PIERRE LIES fewer than twenty miles off Newfoundland's Burin Peninsula, it is historically, linguistically, and administratively French. Moreover, as the atmosphere of the Joinville restaurant suggests, its people have a thoroughly French respect for fine food. Its six major restaurants thrive not just in the tourist season but year-round, serving dishes that the people of Normandy, more than 3,000 miles to the east, have been enjoying for centuries.

29 *Bringing in the nets, Cousin's Shore, P.E.I.*

31 *Cavendish, P.E.I.*

SURF ROARS AT CAVENDISH, Prince Edward Island. The island is so intensely cultivated that its only untamed wilderness is the Gulf itself, and the Gulf is wildest where it batters the beaches, cliffs, dunes, and spits of the north shore. The shaping of this coast is the work of an ancient and intricate conspiracy of winds, tides, ice, ocean, and river currents. The sandstone in the sea-crumbled cliffs is 250 million years old, but the arrangement of beaches and dunes is always newer than the newest sunrise.

Somewhere out there beyond those rollers lie the remains of the *Marco Polo.* Built in Saint John, NB,

she set a world speed record in 1852 by sailing from England to Australia in sixty-eight days, but in 1883 she foundered on a sandbar off Cavendish, and that was the end of her. Cavendish, however, has a more gentle distinction. It's where Lucy Maud Montgomery lived when she wrote *Anne of Green Gables,* and the Green Gables house, which she immortalized, is now a museum. Her grave is in Cavendish cemetery. So are the graves of twenty-one American sailors who drowned in the 'Yankee gale' of 1851. It destroyed 175 New England fishing boats.

32 & 33 (overleaf) *Victoria, P.E.I.*

THESE GENTLE MEADOWS and rolling farmlands lie on the southern coast, facing Northumberland Strait. From Victoria the Bonshaw Hills Trail leads hikers through more farms and, rare today on the Island, cool forests.

30 (left) *De Sable, P.E.I.*

IT MAY NOT BE A POT OF GOLD, but this farm at De Sable is typical of scenes that once inspired a songwriter to come up with, 'Prince Edward Island is heaven to me.'

34 *Blessing of the fleet, Rustico, P.E.I.*

OFF RUSTICO ON THE NORTH SHORE of Prince Edward Island, a priest's robe billows in a Gulf gust as he blesses the fishing fleet. Fish and tourists are keys to Rustico's economy, and it's the fish who lure many of the tourists. By 1980, fifty licensed fishermen in tiny Rustico were still hauling in up to 1.5 million tons a year, and annual landings fetched close to a million dollars, mostly for lobster.

Fishermen also earn money taking groups of tourists out to fish the Gulf. The highway that links the world-famous beaches of Prince Edward Island National Park passes through Rustico, bringing tens of thousands of tourists in search of everything from toothpaste to a twenty-dollar lobster plate, from hamburgers to hand-lined mackerel aboard the boat of an authentic 'character', from a bottle of beer at the big,

thriving Legion hall to a bottle of Scotch from the small, thriving liquor store.

The deluge, however, has not drowned Rustico's character. First settled by pioneers from France, and then by Acadians whom the British had expelled from Nova Scotia, Rustico did gradually lose its language, but not its sense of humour, its generosity, its neighbourliness or, above all, its religion. The Church taught Rustico endurance.

35 (right) *Sorting cranberries, Rustico, P.E.I.*

WITH THE SUN WARMING your hands and back, sorting cranberries within earshot of the Gulf at Rustico, Prince Edward Island, isn't bad work at all. It looks as though it may even keep you young.

37 *Bay St Lawrence, N.S.*

BAY ST LAWRENCE is just about the most northern village in Cape Breton. Caught between the highlands on one hand and the ocean on the other, it inspires intense loyalty among its people.

36 (left) *Freetown, P.E.I.*

'IT IS THE BEST-TEMPERED region one can possibly see...' marvelled Jacques Cartier when he landed on Prince Edward Island. That was during his first Gulf-probing voyage in 1534. He found nothing so cultivated as this farmland near Freetown, but he knew a good thing when he saw it. He cruised part of the north and west shores, went ashore a few times, saw some timid Indians, and observed that, 'All this coast is low and flat but the finest land one can see, and full of beautiful trees and meadows.' He pushed west, then north toward Gaspé, and never knew that this attractive country he had found was in fact an island.

39 *Cormorants*

CORMORANTS HAVE ENDURED bad press for centuries. Their gluttony inspired Shakespeare to make them symbols of greed, devouring even Time. In *Paradise Lost*, John Milton said Satan 'sat like a Cormorant...devising Death.' Percé fishermen call the cormorant a 'snaky beast' and fishermen through-out the Gulf have a low opinion of him. Biologists claim cormorants do little economic damage, but fishermen nevertheless see this low-flying, deep-diving, web-footed, and super-efficient 'sea raven' as a competitor. These devilish fellows (above) perch near Pictou, Nova Scotia, on Northumberland Strait.

38 (left) *Skinner's Pond, P.E.I.*

THE GULF OFFERS other harvests than fish. At Skinner's Pond, northwestern Prince Edward Island, fishermen gather the Irish moss that autumn storms have hurled on the beach. Plants at nearby Minine-gash buy, dry and package this seaweed, then sell it for use in cooking, textile sizing and the making of products ranging from cosmetics to commercial ice cream.

AS MANY AS TWO MILLION harp seals ride ice floes southward from the Arctic for more than a thousand miles each winter to reach their whelping territory. When the massive migration reaches the northern tip of Newfoundland, the herds split. Some continue down the east coast of Newfoundland. Others stay aboard the ice that's sliding through the Strait of Belle Isle and eventually whelp just north of the Magdalen Islands. Seal-hunters there often need no boats. They simply walk across the ice. By spring, the seals are moving north again, with the young ones already on their own but trailing the adults.

40 (left) *Harp seal pup on Gulf ice*

A LIGHTHOUSE CONFRONTS the Gulf near Chéticamp on Cape Breton Island's spectacular—and spectacularly treacherous—north-west coast. Chéti-
41 *Chéticamp, N.S.*

camp is on the Cabot Trail, one of the most beautiful seaside drives in North America. For sailors the outlook is less pleasing.

42 *Tanker wreck, Canso, N.S.*

A ROCK-SKEWERED OIL TANKER breaks up near Nova Scotia's Strait of Canso, the narrowest and most southerly entrance to the Gulf. The Strait of Canso is a gully that separates mainland Nova Scotia from Cape Breton Island. Massive, barge-like ferries used to carry entire railroad trains across the Strait, but in August 1955 the Canso Causeway opened. It's 218 feet deep and 4,300 feet long, one of the world's biggest causeways.

Entering the Gulf through the Strait of Canso, shipping must submit to what's called a 'vessel traffic management system'. There's a system, too, to guide the vessels to and from the Gulf on the St Lawrence River. For westbound shipping, it starts south of Sept-Iles and continues upriver for more than 400 miles to Montreal. Pointe-au-Père (Father Point), 185 miles downstream from Quebec City, is on this route. It was just off Pointe-au-Père, on 29 May 1914, that the *Storstad*, a Norwegian freighter, rammed the *Empress of Ireland*, a 14,191-ton liner of the Canadian Pacific Steamship Co. In the worst marine disaster in Canadian history, the *Empress of Ireland* sank, and took 1,014 lives with her, cruel proof of the constant need for traffic management.

43 *Pugwash, N.S.*

THE SINKING SUN makes Pugwash rosy. This town (population, 644) on the Nova Scotian shore of Northumberland Strait, has street signs in both English and Gaelic, and whoops it up in a Scottish way during its own Gathering of the Clans each 1 July. Cyrus W. Eaton, railroad tycoon and legendary US financier, came from Pugwash and organized the world-famous Pugwash Thinkers Conferences.

44 *Meat Cove, N.S.*

YOU CAN'T DRIVE MUCH FURTHER out on Cape Breton's finger than Bay St Lawrence—except to go to Meat Cove. The road to Meat Cove is a shocker for motorists. It twists, swings and humps round the edge of dizzying cliffs. Far below, where the sea roars, lie rusty chunks of smashed autos. It's not only offshore that the Gulf makes wrecks.

45 (right) *Cap-Rouge, N.S.*

AT CAP-ROUGE on the Cabot Trail, Cape Breton Island, the Gulf foams ashore, and sculpts the rock.

FIVE MILES UP the Mabou River from the Gulf, in western Cape Breton Island, the undulating remnants of ancient mountains loom in autumn over cultivated greensward. Looking at this picture, it's easy to believe the forest is reclaiming farmland that the pioneers cleared during decade after decade of bone-numbing labour. Cape Breton boasts no first-class soil; but then the Highlands and western islands of Scotland were not an agricultural paradise either, and it was chiefly Roman Catholic Scots who first settled Inverness County. Despite the odds, they turned some of it into passable farmland.

The mood of Mabou is still Highland Scots, and farmers still raise sheep and dairy cattle there. In recent years, Dutch farmers have proved that they, too, can carve good livings out of the so-so soil.

47 (right) *Campbellton, N.B.*

AT CAMPBELLTON, the commercial heart of New Brunswick's north shore, mist wreathes Sugarloaf, a mass of volcanic rock 305 meters high.

46 *Mabou Highlands, Cape Breton, N.S.*

48 *Chéticamp, N.S.*

FOURTEEN FRENCH-SPEAKING Acadian families, most of them exiles from mainland Nova Scotia, settled here at Chéticamp on the Gulf coast of Cape Breton Island in 1785–86. Their priests often disliked the place but loved the people. In 1809 Father François Lejamtel, a French-born missionary, wrote that 'they could not be more charitable towards one another. They have great piety, and it would be a pity not to promote and sustain their zeal. They are very generous to the priests who serve them. . . . I had come to them by land and water, crossing the island of Cape Breton, with two Indians. They did not want me to return the same way, saying that it was too hard on me; and they fitted out a vessel at their expense to bring me back to Arischat. . . If a missionary had come to Chéticamp last autumn, he would have suffered from neither hunger nor cold.' More than 1,000 people live there now, and Chéticamp is a centre of Acadian culture in Cape Breton.

49 *River John, N.S.*

NEAR RIVER JOHN, Pictou County, N.S., sweet farmland stretches toward Northumberland Strait, the great neck of the greater Gulf. Pictou County proudly saw (and sees) itself as the historic New World gateway for pioneering Scots, but the pioneers of River John were about as Scottish as Alpine yodelling. Their roots were in Montbeliard, now in eastern France but once a Huguenot refuge belonging to the dukes of Württemberg. After religious persecution in the 1750s, certain families of Montbeliard rafted down the Rhine, reached England, sailed the Atlantic, and settled at Lunenburg County, N.S.

In the 1780s, George and John Patriquin, with a few others, drifted from there to Deception River which, perhaps in tribute to John Patriquin, soon became River John.

George Patriquin's five-year-old son, Frederic, was kidnapped by the Micmacs, who spirited him off to deep woods and turned him into the sort of 'White Indian' you see in certain western movies. After his parents had died, he returned to River John, looked around, and disappeared with the Micmacs all over again.

In the Age of Sail, River John blossomed as a builder of ocean-going vessels. Farming, lumber, and lobster still matter. Maybe 500 people live here now.

51 *Richibucto, N.B.*

EVENING PEACE, Kouchibouguac National Park,
near Richibucto on the Gulf shore of New Brunswick.

50 (left) *Shediac, N.B.*

JUST NORTH OF THIS waterfront playground at
Shediac, New Brunswick, lies a river named by Nico-
las Denys, a remarkable luminary in Acadian affairs
for more than half of the seventeenth century. 'I have
named this river the River of Cocagne, because I
found there so much with which to make good cheer
during the eight days which bad weather obliged me
to remain here,' Denys wrote. 'All my people were so
surfeited with game and fish that they wished no
more, whether wild geese, ducks, teal, plover, snipe
large and small, pigeons, hares, partridges, young
partridges, salmon, trout, mackerel, smelt, oysters,
and other kinds of good fish. All that I can tell you of
it is this, that our dogs lay beside the meat and fish, so
much were they satiated with it. The country there is
as pleasing as the good cheer.' The neighbourhood
still pleases a lot of people—more than 350,000 visitors every summer.

52 (left) *St-Edouard, N.B.*

THESE LOBSTER POTS and buoys happen to be on the New Brunswick side of Northumberland Strait, but you'll find similar scenes in village after village in each of the five provinces that encircle, endure and exploit the Gulf. 'I don't eat bugs,' said a Prairie farmer when offered a boiled lobster. But *Homarus americanus*, the kind of lobster the Gulf grows, is nevertheless the most highly prized creature in the sea, the favourite seafood of gourmets the world over. The restaurant price of a lobster dinner suggests the brute is scarcely a dietary staple for anyone, but as an *economic* staple, lobsters have been doing their bit for the people of the Gulf since before fishing boats had engines.

53 *Caraquet, N.B.*

RAIMONDO DE SONCINO told the Duke of Milan by mail in 1497 that John Cabot had discovered that the Atlantic Ocean, off what's now Newfoundland, was so 'swarming with fish' that they could be taken 'not only with the net, but with buckets let down with a stone. . . .' But Cabot had slipped across the Cabot Strait to Cape Breton Island without ever knowing that off his starboard beam lay the immense Gulf with its own fertile shallows, sea pastures, and an Eldorado of fish. When Cartier felt out the Gulf thirty-seven years later, Basques, Bretons, and possibly fishermen from other European countries had already beaten him to it. One sometimes imagines fishermen hailing the vessels of the official explorers and shouting, 'What kept you?' On the Gulf's northern (Quebec) shore, Cartier unexpectedly met a fishing boat from La Rochelle, a port down the French coast from his home town, St Malo.

Thus, when Jean-Baptiste-Antoine Ferland, a Montreal-born priest, visited Gaspé in the late nineteenth century, the Gulf had been fished commercially for more than three centuries. Yet, he wrote, 'It is the land of the codfish! Your eyes and nose and tongue and throat and ears as well, soon make you realize that in the peninsula of Gaspé, the codfish forms the basis alike of food and amusements, of business and general talk, of regrets, hope, good luck, everyday life—I would almost be ready to say of existence itself.'

And not only the codfish. Caraquet, New Brunswick, which is just across Chaleur Bay from Gaspé, also harvests and freezes haddock, mackerel, and sole. Oysters, clams, and lobster contribute to the economy, too.

The main origin of Caraquet's roughly 3,000 people is Norman, with an infusion of Canadian Acadian, and Jersey French, as well as native Indian and some English.

54 *Hibernation, Robichaud, N.B.*

55 *Grey day at Eel River Crossing, Chaleur Bay, N.B.*

57 *Restoring light beacons, Shippegan, N.B.*

NEAR SHIPPEGAN, New Brunswick, airborne workers serve seagoing workers by tending navigational beacons. The Gulf is a huge fishery for its own seafarers but it's also a funnel that draws vessels from the world's busiest ocean into the heart of the world's richest continent. Some coastline has barely changed since Jacques Cartier first saw it. So it's still a wilderness. But the Gulf is also a *marked* wilderness. Beacons, bells, buoys, lights, signals, warnings, all manner of anchor-bound and land-bound declarations inform the myriad vessels that track the timeless Gulf for gain. From the Strait of Belle Isle, the Gulf's northernmost entrance, a ship can sail inland on the St Lawrence system for more than two thousand miles, all the way to Duluth, Minnesota. Going the other way, the distance from Shippegan to Bristol, England—if you use the Strait of Belle Isle as your exit from the Gulf—is only about 2,370 miles. But perhaps you're bound from Shippegan to Lisbon. Use the Cabot Strait. You'll sail scarcely 2,450 miles. If you duck south through the Canso Strait, you need sail a mere 1,500 miles to reach Savannah, Georgia.

56 (left) *Chatham, N.B.*

AT CHATHAM, New Brunswick, eel nets dangle beside the most beautifully named river in Canada, if not the world—the 'Miramichi' (Meer-a-mi-shee).

58 *St Edouard, N.B.*

59 (right) *Sault-au-Mouton, Qué.*

WHITE WATER ROARS at Sault-au-Mouton, downriver from Tadoussac on the North Shore of the St Lawrence River.

60 *Acadian Village, N.B.*

BETWEEN CARAQUET and Grand-Anse, New Brunswick, on Chaleur Bay, pioneer Acadia lives again in the Acadian Historical Village. There could scarcely be a more appropriate spot to celebrate an irrepressible culture. In 1755 Britain expelled roughly 14,000 Roman Catholic, French-speaking Acadians from land in the Maritimes that they had peacefully cultivated for generations. Later in the century, how-ever, hundreds of Acadians endured a painful pilgrim-age back to the Maritimes. One of the areas where they once again sank roots was the coast of north-eastern New Brunswick. The reconstructed village demonstrates pioneer skills and amusements, and each summer attracts more than 100,000 visitors, many of them from Louisiana, France, and Quebec, as well as the Atlantic provinces.

61 *Gaspé, Qué.*

THIS MONUMENT AT GASPÉ, Quebec, commem-
orates Jacques Cartier's landing on a summer day 450
years ago—24 July 1534—and his taking possession of
the neighbourhood in the name of the King of France.
Cartier also erected a wooden cross, thirty feet high,
and then pushed on to further discoveries in the Gulf.

62 *St Denis, Qué.*

EIGHTY MILES DOWN from Quebec City on the south bank of the St Lawrence in Kamouraska County sits St-Denis, resort town, farming centre, and once the home of Jean Charles Chapais, a Father of Confederation in Canada.

63 *St-Joseph-de-la-Rive, Qué.*

FROM ST-JOSEPH-DE-LA-RIVE, Quebec, terminal for ferries to Ile aux Coudres in the tidal reaches of the river, the view of the rolling Gulf-bound stream is peerless.

BOATYARD AT TADOUSSAC, mouth of the Saguenay River, Quebec. The first French visitors to Tadoussac arrived 449 years ago when, on 1 September 1535, Jacques Cartier sailed into the mouth of the Saguenay. That's 130-odd miles below Quebec City. The hills near Tadoussac are curvaceous, and the spot gets its name from an Indian word for 'breasts'. It overlooks the Saguenay at the point where the river plunges into the St Lawrence from the north. Inland lies a country that the Indians told Cartier was the fabulous Kingdom of the Saguenay. As Cartier sailed away, 'we...discovered a species of fish which none of us had ever seen or heard of. This fish is as large as a porpoise but has no fin. It is very similar to a greyhound about the body and head and is as white as snow, without a spot on it. Of these there are a very large number in this river, living between the salt and the fresh water.' Even now, visitors marvel at the beluga whales near the mouth of the Saguenay, and Tadoussac remains one of the most historic spots in Canada.

65 (right) *Ile aux Coudres, Qué.*

THE DESAGNÉ WINDMILL, 207 years old, is one of several historic monuments on tiny (thirteen square miles) Ile aux Coudres. Named by Cartier for the abundance of hazelnut trees he found there on 7 September 1535, Ile aux Coudres is still a true island, without bridge or causeway to the nearby north shore of the St Lawrence. A ferry links it to Saint-Joseph-de-la-Rive. Like the bigger Ile d'Orléans, further upriver, Ile aux Coudres has a powerful flavour of rural life in 18th-century New France.

64 *Tadoussac, Qué.*

67 (right) *St-Roch-des-Aulnets, Qué.*

THE DAY IS BENIGN, the streets silent, at Saint-Roch-des-Aulnets on the south shore of the St Lawrence River. It lies roughly midway between Quebec City and Rivière-du-Loup.

66 *Grand Hotel, Tadoussac, Qué.*

NEAR HERE, in 1600, Pierre Chauvin built the first permanent house in Canada.

Across the cove from the Grand Hotel at Tadoussac, tables await summer visitors.

68 *Baie-St-Paul, Qué.*

NO LANDSCAPE THAT FLANKS the St Lawrence system is more mellow-looking than that of Baie-Saint-Paul. It sits on the north shore of the river, well below Quebec City but well above the mouth of the Saguenay. The river already feels the tides here, and broadens as it slides toward the Gulf.

69 *Rivière-du-Moulin, Qué.*

FAR UP THE SAGUENAY—past Baie Eternité, not to mention Baie des Ha! Ha!—Rivière-du-Moulin rattles down through the outskirts of Chicoutimi to join the mightier river as it rushes south to the St Lawrence between towering cliffs.

70 & 71 (overleaf) *Bird Rock Island, Qué.*

IF YOU'RE INCLINED towards sleep-walking, you wouldn't want to live at 'the loneliest lighthouse in Canada' on Bird Rock. A rotten staircase still clings to one of the one-hundred-foot cliffs, but since 1966 helicopters have brought supplies and relief to the lightkeepers. Haven for birds, menace to vessels, Bird Rock looks like a platform that's been cut adrift from its neighbours among the Magdalen Islands, seventeen miles away. It's a 6.2-acre lump of sandstone.

For anyone with vertigo, the cliffs are uninviting, but gannets find them highly satisfactory. So do puffins, murres, sea pigeons, and half a dozen other varieties. Spring sees up to 100,000 birds here.

Conquering boredom is the modern problem, but in an earlier time a hideous curse seemed to afflict the men who dared to live here. The first lighthouse keeper went mad. The second, with his son, was lost on the ice. The third, with *his* son in turn, was killed when a keg of gunpowder exploded. The fourth was nearly killed by the fog gun. One of their successors remarked of his own eleven-year stay, 'I didn't miss it when I left. Not one bit.'

THE *FORT MINGAN* pauses in fog at Harrington-Harbour before shoving off for other isolated villages on Quebec's Lower North Shore. The north shore of the Gulf is also the south coast of much of Quebec, and has a lot in common with the south coast of Newfoundland; it was Newfoundlanders who established Harrington-Harbour as a fishing community in 1875, and most of the shore is English-speaking. The similarities to coastal Newfoundland do not stop there. Both coasts endure many shortages—of roads, soil, growing weather, fresh food, job opportunities, good schools, municipal services—and enjoy one abundance. The abundance is fish. It has been said of the Lower North Shore that if it weren't for the fish, nobody would be living there. The fishermen mostly use small boats, cod traps, gill nets, hand lines, and jiggers. They manage to haul in eight million pounds of cod per year, but higher-priced salmon, sea trout, and shellfish are also important to their survival.

73 (right) *St-Omar, Gaspé, Qué.*

THE OWNER OF THIS BOAT on the Gaspé coast can haul her in like clothes on a line. He can board her without wetting his feet. The Gaspé Peninsula has been a hangout for ingenious sailors for nearly five centuries. It was among the first parts of Canada to be visited by Basque, Norman, Spanish, and Portuguese fishermen, and may take its name from Portuguese explorer Gaspar Cort-Réal. He might have been in these parts as early as 1500. On the other hand, the name could also come from *gespeg*, Indian for 'end of the world'.

72 *Harrington-Harbour, Qué.*

75 *Anticosti, Qué.*

ANTICOSTI ISLAND, mostly deserted, boasts several secret, spectacular waterfalls.

74 (left) *Cap des Rosiers, Qué.*

A BRITISH NAVAL OFFICER reported to the First Lord of the Admiralty in 1828 that there were still no lighthouses anywhere in the Gulf, and deplored the number of wrecks on the coasts. It wasn't until 1857 that the government erected four lighthouses. The tallest of these was a solid 112-foot tower at Cap des Rosiers, built like a fortress to withstand weather's fiercest sieges. Set fifty feet back from the cliff, the foundation was eight feet deep. At the base the walls were more than seven feet thick, and they tapered to a three-foot thickness at the top. More than a century after its construction, it was still in good shape.

76 *Puffins*

THE PUFFIN WEARS three colours on its beak, yellow, blue and red. This tropical effect, in the decidedly untropical Gulf, is seasonal and sexual. The colours are breeding plumage. In the fall, puffins shed their bright beak embellishments to reveal a smaller, duller bill. In short, these birds have moulting noses.

Puffins are nosy in other ways as well. They're curious, unwary, gregarious. In the Gulf, they breed on Quebec's Lower North Shore, and at Anticosti Island, Bonaventure Island, and the Magdalens. They catch fish by landing on the water, diving underwater, then using both their feet and wings to pursue their catch. They've been called 'flying submarines'. That funny-looking beak enables a puffin to carry home as many as eight small, whole herring at a time.

77 *Whalebones and deer, Anticosti, Qué.*

UPRIVER FROM HERE, where the southbound Saguenay joins the eastbound St Lawrence, where the water is deep and icy and the feeding plentiful, beluga whales still appear often enough to bedazzle whale-watchers who pay to go out on boats to see them cavort. Belugas have enjoyed these parts for roughly ten thousand years.

Henri Menier, the multi-millionaire 'Chocolate King of France', bought Anticosti Island for $125,000 in 1895 and, with the help of his equally autocratic cohort, Georges Martin-Zédé, tried to turn this gigantic wilderness holding into a combination of private game preserve, feudal principality, and utopia for aristocrats, artisans, and peasants.

In 1896, Menier bought 110 male and 110 female white-tailed Virginia deer and let them loose on Anti-

costi. Most of his efforts to set up animal populations fizzled, but this one worked too well. With few predators to thin them out, the deer proliferated so fast that, according to one islander, winter conditions alone killed no less than 20,000 in 1955. Compared with that, the kill by hunters was trifling. By the 1980s it was likely that Anticosti, with a human population of only 300, had a deer population of 100,000.

Menier spent millions on his bizarre scheme, and one of his more expensive fiascos was the 'model settlement' of Bai Ste Claire, named after his mother. By the early 1900s, more than 220 people lived in this handsome village but they drifted away until only a few deserted headstones remained to bear witness to the dream.

79 *Cod, Anticosti, Qué.*

HUNG OUT TO DRY, codfish smell in the breeze off Jacques Cartier Passage at MacDonald River, Anticosti Island. Even before Cartier passed this way, Europeans dried fish on Gulf shores. Thanks to this simple method of curing, and preservation in salt, the cod trade flourished and spanned the Atlantic. It fed the Roman Catholic peoples of Europe and the slaves of the West Indies. It brought salt, rum and molasses from the Caribbean to New England, the Maritimes and Newfoundland; spawned the famous schooner fleets of Lunenburg, N.S., and Gloucester, Mass.; and, for centuries, brought both money and midwinter nourishment to the people of the Gulf.

78 (left) *Dried caplin, Anticosti, Qué.*

THE BEST, CONCISE definition of this fish, so crucial to the fisheries, is in the *Dictionary of Newfoundland English* (1982): 'A small, iridescent deep-water fish *(Mallotus villosus)* like a smelt, which, followed by the cod, appears inshore during June and July to spawn along the beaches, and is netted for bait, for manuring the fields, or dried, salted, smoked or frozen for eating.' Fishermen net caplin to catch cod.

81 *On board the* Fort Mingan

WEATHER PERMITTING, the *Fort Mingan* makes weekly round trips between Rimouski, 180 miles downriver from Quebec on the south shore of the St Lawrence, and Blanc-Sablon, the uttermost Quebec community on the coast of 'the land God gave to Cain'. It was Jacques Cartier who applied that immortal description to the north shore of the Gulf. Having seen its glacier-scraped, sea-scoured granite and its scrubby, twisted evergreens in 1534, he said it 'should not be called the New Land, being composed of stones and horrible ragged rocks; for along the whole of the north shore, I did not see one cart-load of earth and yet I landed in many places. Except at Blanc-Sablon there is nothing but moss and short, stunted shrub.'

The meagre coastal settlements endure a near-Arctic isolation, making the *Fort Mingan* and her crew crucial to their well-being. She brings them cargo, passengers, friends, relatives, news. As long as the Gulf's ice-free, she rarely stops chugging. After all, from Rimouski to Blanc-Sablon and back again is but a little matter of 1,200 miles.

80 (left) *Shipwreck, Anticosti, Qué.*

ANTICOSTI ISLAND has a gruesome maritime history. Its currents, winds and reefs have been a sailor's nightmare for centuries. In the mid-1800s, the square-timber industry turned Quebec City into a world port, and every summer roughly 2,000 ships had to make their perilous way past Anticosti. In the 1870s alone, the limestone reefs snared 106 ships; and since the late 1600s at least 400 vessels have foundered there. Thousands of castaways have been swept ashore, and the tales of starvation and cannibalism are as grim as any you'll find in shipwreck history. Sable Island, out in the open ocean off Nova Scotia, is notorious as 'The Graveyard of the Atlantic'; but for sheer grisliness its record has nothing on 'The Graveyard of the Gulf'.

82 *Barn at Saint-Jean-Port-Joli, Quebec, on the south shore of the St Lawrence River, below Quebec City*

83 *Cap Tourmente, Qué.*

EVERY FALL, roughly 100,000 snow geese pause at Cap Tourmente during their migration from breeding grounds in the Canadian Arctic to wintering grounds in Virginia and North Carolina. In spring, on their way back north, they again drop in at the Cap Tourmente National Wildlife Area for a few weeks. The park is about 35 miles below Quebec City on the north shore of the river. A snow goose, while feeding, makes what one eminent bird-watcher has described as 'gabbling and groaning sounds'. If you multiply the gabbles and groans by 100,000, you get a powerful chorus.

84 *Gannets*

GANNETS ARE TWICE as big as herring gulls and almost as big as geese. While fishing, they're spectacular dive bombers. They winter on the coast of the American South and return to Gulf sanctuaries such as Bonaventure Island in early spring.

85 (right) *Ile d'Orléans, Qué.*

THE FLAIR is decidedly French on Ile d'Orléans, even on a barn wall.

86 (left) *Ile d'Orléans, Qué.*

A MAN OF ILE D'ORLEANS and proud of it, a man
of Old Quebec.

87(a) *Lobsters (see plate 52)*   87(b) *Carleton, Anticosti, Qué.*

89 *Amqui, Qué.*

QUEBEC BARNS HAVE a certain élan. This one's at Amqui, inland from the south shore of the St Lawrence. Amqui is on the Matapedia River, which flows southeast to the Restigouche Estuary, leading to Chaleur Bay and on to the Gulf.

88 (left) *Ste-Anne-de-Beaupré, Qué.*

EVERY YEAR, hundreds of thousands of people flock to the faith-healing shrine at Ste-Anne-de-Beaupré, 30-odd kilometres downriver from Quebec City. Some are merely tourists, some are devout, some yearn for a heaven-sent cure. For three centuries, especially during the week leading up to the feast day of Saint Anne on 26 July, pilgrims have been making their way to her shrine on the Beaupré Coast of the St Lawrence River. It is said that Breton sailors erected a chapel here in 1658 to honor Saint Anne. They'd prayed to her for salvation while their ship was in distress. It is also said that her intercession cured a man of lumbago while he was helping build the chapel. Only seven years later, in 1665, Marie de l'Incarnation, founder of the Ursuline Convent, described a church of St-Anne-de-Beaupré where the blind recovered their sight, the paralytic walked once more, and the diseased became well.

90 *Ile d'Orléans, Qué.*

JUST BELOW QUEBEC CITY, Isle d'Orléans lies in the St Lawrence and basks in a glow of history. The entire island is an official historic region, and a visit there is as close as you can come to stepping into the farm life of 18th-century Quebec. Galleries, theatres and restaurants have taken over some barns and houses, with their Norman-style roofs, but others still serve rural families as they did two or three centuries ago. The islanders are history-proud, just as some women are house-proud, and their old stone churches are among the most beautiful in Quebec. The island's wild grapes so impressed Cartier that he called it 'Bacchus', for the Roman god of wine, then decided he'd be smarter to name it after King Francis I's son, the Duke of Orléans. At Ile d'Orléans, saltwater tides roll upriver to meet freshwater currents and, in that sense, the cigar-shaped island marks the upriver limit of the Gulf of St Lawrence.

91 *Fishermen, Percé, Qué.*

92 *Percé, Qué.*

AT PERCÉ ON THE GASPÉ peninsula, the last light of evening throws a glow over the Gulf, fishing village, harbour, rock, and cross. Like every other European on his way upriver, Francois-Xavier de Laval de Montigny, the Jesuit vicar-general of the Pope in New France, had to cross the Gulf. He paused at Percé to celebrate his first Mass on Canadian soil, then plunged inland. That was in 1659. Five years later he became Bishop of Quebec and by the time he retired in 1688—the year, incidentally, that William of Orange became king of England—he had earned his place as a giant of early Canadian history.

93 *Port-au-Persil, Qué.*

BEYOND THE BLUE HORIZON at Port-au-Persil lies the huge Gulf and beyond that, the seven seas.

94 & 95 (overleaf) *Percé, Qué.*

PERCÉ, AT THE EASTERN TIP of the Gaspé Peninsula, may well be the most famous rock in Atlantic Canada. Beloved by cormorants, puffins, gannets, gulls and tourists, it's been a bird sanctuary since 1919. In the usual view, you see Percé's entire length. It is a slab of limestone 1,500 feet long, 288 feet high, and pierced *(percé)* by an archway-shaped opening that's sixty feet high by one hundred feet wide. In full profile then Percé Rock looks like an aircraft carrier with a gaping hole at the waterline. This end-on view shows the slab brooding as night descends, and proves that Percé Rock is still impressive from any angle, just as it was when Samuel de Champlain named it almost four centuries ago.

96 *Rivière-du-Loup, Qué.*

STEEPLES AT DUSK proclaim the ancient aspiration of establishing a Christian civilization on the edge of a vast, hard, cold wilderness. The scene is near Rivière-du-Loup (Wolf River), which takes its name from the packs of timber wolves that once haunted the neighbourhood. Rivière-du-Loup is 120 miles closer to the Gulf than Quebec City, and sits on the south bank of the St Lawrence. The river is still tidal here, and fifteen miles wide, but it has begun to narrow into the businesslike waterway that carries world shipping to the heart of the continent.

Bibliography

Books

Andrieux, Jean-Pierre. *Shipwreck!* Beamsville, Ontario, W.F. Rannie, 1975.

Berrill, Michael and Deborah. *A Sierra Club Naturalist's Guide to the North Atlantic Coast.* San Francisco, Sierra Club Books, 1981.

Bird, Will R. ed. *Atlantic Anthology.* Toronto, McClelland & Stewart Ltd., 1959.

—*This is Nova Scotia.* Toronto, The Ryerson Press, 1955.

Bruce, Harry. Lifeline, *The Story of the Atlantic Ferries and Coastal Boats.* Toronto, Macmillan of Canada, 1977.

Colombo, John Robert. *Colombo's Canadian References.* Toronto, Oxford University Press, 1976.

Creighton, Donald. *The Empire of the St. Lawrence.* Toronto, The MacMillan Company of Canada Ltd., 1956.

Dawson, Samuel Edward. *The Saint Lawrence Basin.* Toronto, McClelland, Goodchild and Stewart Ltd., 1905.

Dennis, Clara. *More About Nova Scotia.* Toronto, The Ryerson Press, 1937.

Department of Fisheries and Oceans. *Sailing Directions, Gulf and River St. Lawrence, Fourth Edition.* Ottawa, Department of Fisheries and Oceans, 1980.

Engel, Marian, J.A. Kraulis. *The Islands of Canada.* Edmonton, Hurtig Publishers Ltd., 1981.

Godfrey, W. Earl. *The Birds of Canada.* Ottawa, Queen's Printer for Canada, 1966.

Grolier Society of Canada. *Encyclopedia Canadiana.* Ottawa, The Grolier Society of Canada, 1963.

Hannon, Leslie F. *The Discoverers, An Illustrated History.* Toronto/Montreal, McClelland and Stewart Ltd., 1971.

Harrington, Michael. *Sea Stories From Newfoundland.* Toronto, The Ryerson Press, 1958.

Hoffman, Bernard G. *Cabot to Cartier, Sources for a Historical Ethnography of Northeastern North America 1497-1550.* Toronto, University of Toronto Press, 1961.

Horwood, Harold. *Newfoundland.* Toronto, Macmillan of Canada, 1969.

Johnston, A.A. *A History of the Catholic Church in Eastern Nova Scotia.* Antigonish, N.S., St. Francis Xavier University Press, Vol. I, 1960; Vol. II, 1972.

Lefolii, Ken. *The St. Lawrence Valley.* Toronto, NSL Natural Science of Canada Ltd., 1970.

Lemoine, Sir James. *Chronicles of the St. Lawrence.* Montreal, Dawson Bros., 1878.

MacKay, Donald. *Anticosti, The Untamed Island.* Toronto/Montreal, McGraw-Hill Ryerson Ltd., 1979.

MacLennan, Hugh. *The Watch That Ends the Night.* Toronto, Macmillan of Canada, 1958.

Mélançon, Claude. *Percé and Bonaventure Island's seabirds.* Montreal, Editions du Jour, 1963.

Mowat, Farley. *A Whale For The Killing.* Toronto, McClelland & Stewart, 1972.

Moyles, R.G. *Complaints is many and various but the odd divil likes it.* Toronto, Peter Martin Associates, 1975.

Patterson, George. *A History of the County of Pictou.* Montreal, Dawson Brothers, 1877.

Reader's Digest Association (Canada) Ltd. *Canadian Book of the Road.* The Readers' Digest Association (Canada) Ltd., in conjunction with the Canadian Automobile Association, 1979.

—*Explore Canada.* The Reader's Digest Association (Canada) Ltd., in conjunction with the Canadian Automobile Association, 1974.

—*Scenic Wonders of Canada.* The Readers' Digest Association (Canada) Ltd., in conjunction with the Canadian Automobile Association, 1977, 1976.

Russell, Franklin. *The Atlantic Coast.* Toronto, NSL Natural Science of Canada Ltd., 1970.

—*The Sea Has Wings.* New York, E.P. Dutton Company, Inc., 1973.

—*Searchers at the Gulf.* New York, W.W. Norton & Company, Inc., 1970.

Rutledge, Joseph Lister. *Century of Conflict.* Toronto, Doubleday Canada Ltd., 1956.

Story, G.M., W.J. Kirwin, J.D.A. Widdowson. *Dictionary of Newfoundland English.* Toronto, University of Toronto Press, 1982.

Story, Norah. *The Oxford Companion to Canadian History and Literature.* Oxford University Press (Canadian Branch), 1967.

University of Toronto Press. *Dictionary of Canadian Biography.* Toronto, University of Toronto Press, Vol. I, 1966; Vol. II, 1969.

Warburton, A.B. *A History of Prince Edward Island.* Saint John, N.B., Barnes & Company Ltd., 1923.

Witney, Dudley. *The Lighthouse.* Toronto, McClelland and Stewart Ltd., 1975.

Booklets

The Lower North Shore, Towards the future. Quebec, Conseil exécutif, Développement culturel, 1980.

Articles

Bruce, Harry. "Claws A Sequel to Jaws?" *En Route,* July/August 1976.

—"The Magdalens." *The Canadian/Star Weekly,* 4-11 March 1967.

—"Rustico, P.E.I." *Atlantic Insight,* November 1980.

Bush, Edward F. "The Canadian Lighthouse." *Canadian Historic Sites: Occasional Papers in Archaeology and History—No. 9.* Ottawa, Parks Canada, Indian and Northern Affairs, 1974.

Donham, Parker Barss. "Bay St. Lawrence, N.S." *Atlantic Insight,* June 1980.

Fraser, Winston. "Anticosti: big, unknown, and now a park." *Canadian Geographic* Vol. 103, No. 2, April/May 1983.

Lewis, Blanche McLeod. "Along the North Shore in Cartier's Wake." *Canadian Geographical Journal,* May 1934.

MacKay, Douglas. "Some Fresh Glimpses of a Familiar River." *Canadian Geographical Journal,* August 1930.

Thompson, Colleen. "Acadia's story comes to life." *Atlantic Insight,* November 1979.

Zierler, Amy. "St. Pierre: C'est si bon." *Atlantic Insight,* July 1981.

—"Vikings slept here." *Atlantic Insight,* July 1980.

Index of Places